JAYAN E. ROMESH

A Harmonious Way to Live
In a Changing World

A Metta Library Publication

Published 2018 By Metta Library
www.mettalibrary.com
Cover designed by Linda Stelluti
Book designed by Jayan E. Romesh
ISBN-13: 978-1978326446
ISBN-10: 1978326440

Library of Congress Control Number: 2017918870
CreateSpace Independent Publishing Platform
North Charleston, SC

Acknowledgements

I would like to acknowledge the circumstances, motivations, and people who have awakened my harmonious way of living, guiding the way as my life has unfolded.

It is with the deepest gratitude that I acknowledge and thank Venerable Bhikkhu Bodhi, Dr. Rick Hanson, Marc Allen, Christine Kloser, Kate Batten, Adrianne Ross, Rachel Lewis, Karen Lawrie, and all spiritual teachers for their insights, teachings, and continual encouragement. I especially thank those of you who will learn the lessons in this message and find your harmonious life – wherever you are, whoever you are.

I am also grateful to all the lovely people who supported me with harmonious efforts, transforming the manuscript into this book.

Special thanks to Erin McCabe for editing the manuscript and to Linda Stelluti for the cover design.

Finally, I would like to express my gratitude to my loving mother, Charitha Edirisinghe, my loving wife, Manjula Priyadharshanie, my loving mother in-law Leticia Rajapaksa, and all my loving family members, work colleagues, friends, and readers, without whom this book would not have come into existence. And to the greatest teacher in the world: this harmonious life on Earth.

It is my humble aspiration for you to find this book helpful and for it to provide clear, practical wisdom and tools to find your harmonious way of living in a changing world.

May the merits from this gift of writing bless my late loving father Don Francis Edirisinghe, and my late loving father in-law R.R.W Rajapaksa.

May You All Be Safe, Healthy, Happy, and at Ease.

This Book is Dedicated to

All Peace Loving People

READ THIS FIRST

Just to say thanks for looking inside my book, I would like to give you a FREE Ebook! Contact me at: j.romesh@yahoo.com Or go to: www.mettalibrary.com

May this book bring you a Harmonious Way to Live,

With,

Blessings,

Jayau.

This enlightening book, **"A Harmonious Way to Live, In a Changing World"**, was completed on a weekend. It was in September 2017, and the world was facing many challenges in the form of natural disasters and political conflicts. With compassion, I poured my heart out and completed "A Harmonious Way to Live."

From all my days in Canada, one memory stands out like the rising sun. After losing a game, a minor riot broke out between a group of young hockey fans. I felt a message penetrating my mind and the very depths of my soul; I was in Vancouver, and blessed to be living in such a city. It was a few short years ago that I landed in this city, gloriously freed by more than twenty hours of air travel over sea and land to reach what seemed to be the other side of the planet, Sri Lanka – the pearl of the Indian ocean.

As time passed and the memories from that fateful day began to fade, I developed a strong desire to find and share this message of hope. As time passed, I witnessed the selfless actions of the men and women of Canadian Health Services. This made me ponder many things, and I finally put pen to paper and started to pour out my overflowing love and compassion. The message leapt hot from my heart. It came to me like a flash, but remained incomplete until September, when an increasingly conflicted world emphasized it urgency. Yes, the mindful person is the man who does his work – who lives harmoniously without harming the world around him. This extends to all beings, including the environment.

The point I wish to make is this: the universe will aid you in any endeavour whenever you have harmonious intentions, and will send you an angel of assistance when you need it most. A noble and godlike character is not a result of favour or chance, but is the natural result of harmonious effort. My heart goes out to the men and women who do their services in a Godly manner, a quality so rare that no employer can afford to let these individuals go. So too the man who is tasked with taking harmonious action, and does it with harmony, kindness, compassion and sympathy. They are the men and women who strive to carry on a great cause with hearts alight with compassion. Civilization is one long anxious search for just such individuals, and anything such a person asks shall be granted. He is wanted in every city, town and village. This is the man who against great odds has directed all efforts to serve others and love the world with an open and loving heart. The world will never be harmed by such men and women. The world cries out for such individuals; they are needed more than ever in this changing world. He is the master of his thoughts, the moulder of his character, and the maker and shaper of his environment and destiny. He is the one whose purpose on this planet has become to assist others with harmonious living.

With lack of education in Canada, I have realized that young men do not only need to learn from books, nor instruction about this or that, but must learn to act promptly and seize opportunities to serve the world. Opportunities often do not knock for long, and if men will not act for themselves, what will happen when the benefit of their efforts is for all? The willingness to undertake independent harmonious action has the power to lift your life and carry a message to the world. The form of those who do should be cast in deathless bronze and these statues placed in every college in the land. It is not book learning, but the wisdom to face life which will teach people to be harmless and loyal, to act mindfully, to concentrate their energies, to do all things with harmonious and wholesome intentions, and to ultimately carry "A Harmonious Message" for the benefit of all beings and the environment. It is the ability to concentrate on a thing and do it harmoniously without harming the surrounding world.

Let us drop a tear for the men who strive to carry on a great cause, whose working hours extend beyond the work place, and whose hair is fast turning white with the struggle to withstand the challenges of a modern world.

I wish to speak a word of sympathy for the man who succeeds; the man who, against great odds, has directed the efforts of others, and having succeeded, finds there's nothing in it but bare board and clothes. My heart goes to the man who, when given a task, quietly and patiently takes harmonious action to complete it whole heartedly. He is wanted in every city, town and village – in every office, shop, store and factory. The world cries out for such; he is needed in a conflicted world – a man who can carry "A Message of Harmonious Way to Live."

Part 1

Awakening to the Harmonious Way

2010, Colombo, Sri Lanka.

Well, it wasn't so very long ago – only seven years ago.

I was successful but my life lacked meaning,

I was wealthy but lacked happiness,

I was secure but lacked peace.

Then the dreams began.

Sri Lanka was affected by worldly violence at the time, and I was called to leave my Motherland in search of peace and prosperity. Affected by war, conflicts and economic downturn, I was compelled to travel west. Vancouver was a beautiful land full of opportunities and peace. It truly was glorious and free. I was an engineer of a reputed company in Colombo: forty years old and seeking opportunities to grow and to live a life full of happiness and peace. Deciding to come to Vancouver was an uncertain investment that would cost several thousands of dollars, but I made the choice in search of my unique purpose on this planet. This choice opened the gates to a harmonious path and was the light that guided my way to the message that you now hold in your hands.

In over 20 hours of travel over air, water and land, from dawn to dusk I landed in Vancouver in 2010. I had discovered my home for the rest of the years...

It was a cold winter in Canada, during which I had to struggle with the small amount of funds that remained after my travel expenses and unemployment. My journey had taken me thousands of miles and had left me with only a few hundred dollars. For days I wandered up and down the streets, going into scores of places and asking if they needed "a hand", but "no" was the invariable reply. My unkempt appearance led many to believe I was a refugee from a distant land. But I was not discouraged. I continued to look forward to things changing with harmonious understanding. I heard through a fellow countrymen that assemblers were wanted at a manufacturing facility in Vancouver. I met this person through my harmonious efforts.

"When you have harmonious understanding, harmonious intentions follow,

When you have harmonious intentions, harmonious speech and harmonious action follows,

When you have harmonious actions, harmonious effort follows."

"As one advances confidently with harmonious understanding to live the life which he has found through harmonious way, he will meet with a success unexpected."

My persistence paid off, and they invited me for an interview. I arrived at the door the following morning hours before I was expected for the interview, and was greeted by the plant manager who led me into the interview room. Eager to seize any opportunity at hand, I immediately accepted a position as an assembler in the plant's production line.

"Don't wait for extraordinary opportunities, seize common occasions and make them great with harmonious efforts."

This immediate decision to accept the job offer combined with my continuous goal of whole-hearted action, and the world before me began to make sense.

Safety shoes were compulsory at the work place but I could not afford them, and so I borrowed a pair of shoes from someone I had come to know purely by chance. My successful first day at the plant was a result of my creativity and resourcefulness.

The next few years at the plant presented many challenges as I became familiar with a fast paced, multicultural working environment. I cultivated the methods to handle them effectively through mindful, harmonious intentions of loving kindness and compassion.

Mindfulness is experiencing life as it is nonjudgmentally. Loving kindness is the expression of unconditional love without the expectation of anything in return. True compassion is a genuine concern for others, highlighted with feelings of closeness, empathy, and a sense of responsibility.

I have always gone the extra mile in whatever task I undertook, and have considered it a harmonious effort for a harmonious way of living. Years went by with no apparent change; nothing to bring me nearer to the career goals I had set in my mind.

But something important was happening in my life: I was continuously choosing to experience each day with mindful awareness, and I began to notice subtle changes in my life; I was more patient and less reactive, more open, more aware and more in control of my life. My life flowed harmoniously, despite adversity and human nature presenting unavoidably setbacks here and there.

Every failure, setback and heartache made my journey more interesting. I learned to turn inspiration into action, wisdom, and the power to overcome. I worked to cultivate a mindful way of experiencing pleasure and pain, gain and loss, praise and blame, fame and disrepute, so that these temporary emotional states could not touch my inner stillness. This is the *Harmonious Way to Live*, in a changing world.

"Just as a mighty boulder stirs not with the wind so the wise are never moved either by praise or blame."

- Dhammapada

I made the decision to persevere through every setback and did so with the practice of mindful living. My imagination, kindness and compassion attracted similar minds within and beyond the work place, those who would eventually work with me towards a goal of greater harmony. The combination of knowledge and effort in the spirit of harmony attracted many people, and began to pave the path towards great achievements.

My harmonious efforts were rewarded, both in my personal life and in my work, and I was soon living a more fulfilled life.

"We are what we think,

All that we are arises with our thoughts,

With our thoughts we make the world,

Speak or act with an impure mind,

And trouble will follow you,

As the wheel follows the ox that draws the cart,

Speak or act with a pure mind,

And happiness will follow you,

As your shadow, unshakable."

– Dhammapada

I continued to go the extra mile in my new mindful life, aiming to help others with a sense confidence and generosity. Sending my positive energies outwards also increased my unique talents and personal creativity. I found my work more meaningful and less stressful, which increased my desire to serve and fulfill the labors of love.

My courage, determination, and faith in the importance of a mindful life has played a major role in my own life, and I feel strongly that these benefits will eventually serve the whole world.

"I acted with love in my heart, and behold, Service was joy."

The hard work throughout the past few years produced steady gains, and gradually I overcame my fear of poverty and helplessness.

A portion of my earnings were saved, and the rest was invested in social service for those in need. One such wholehearted service gave birth to Metta Library, a publishing effort that publishes books to enlighten lives. Although I fall back from time to time I now understand the formula to overcome setbacks. In times of trouble I seek guidance through mindful awareness, and do not dwell on the past which is merely a memory. I choose to see the beauty and power of the present moment.

I have come to recognize challenges as gifts; they are opportunities to learn and grow. They provide us with the space to increase acceptance, forgiveness, flexibility, patience, loving kindness, compassion, harmlessness, equanimity and joy.

Genuine boundless love and compassion for all living beings has shown me that life has powerful possibilities in a changing world. I came to feel the connection to all life; and to truly understand the importance of every individual within this interconnectedness. I saw myself in everyone I opened my heart to, interacting from a place of cooperation rather than competition. I felt blessed to be alive. A calm came over me; I felt protected and at peace. In the deepest part of my being, I knew I had nothing to fear. I felt my breath.

Breathing in, I am aware of feeling joy

Breathing out, I am aware of feeling joy

Breathing in, I am aware of feeling happiness

Breathing out, I am aware of feeling happiness

Breathing in, I am aware of my mental formations

Breathing out, I am aware of my mental formations

Breathing in, I am calm with my connection

Breathing out, I am calm with my connection

Practice this way of being connected to everything and notice the peace and happiness that may have eluded you for a lifetime. This peace is part of the oneness you are free to receive.

"If you put your heart on the earth with love and compassion, in serving every creature you will evolve with love, peace, and joy."

I made sure to accept my calmness, as it allowed me to express my creativity freely. It also allowed me to genuinely accept others; it was my greatest power. I was able to alter my thoughts towards things and other persons, which was an important step in creating a harmonious environment. I saw the diversity that has the power to unite us: the fabric of human existence, the key to unity, and the shared sense of purpose with compassion.

I started living in the spirit of wholeness. I saw the beauty of nature and the miracle of our lives on this planet. I was driven to live in a more Earth-friendly manner as a part of this overwhelming oneness; I became an advocate for conservation and moderation. I started taking the time to pick up and recycle trash, and would frequently utilize public transport to carry out my gifts of service. I opted to drive an environmentally friendly automobile, and was even more satisfied to walk in peace to as many places as possible. I felt comfortable in the feeling that my relationship to the universe was harmonized and in tune.

"Happiness is mental harmony."

I have learned to allow the present moment to be as it is, and to accept the impermanent nature of all things and conditions. My thoughts will be constructive, never destructive. My mind will dwell in the present moment and its infinite possibilities; it will not dwell in the illusion of the past. I will seek the association of those who are striving to bring about mindful changes in the world. My realization of our short journey on earth has given me a harmonious way to live, and to carry "A Harmonious Message to a Changing World."

A Harmonious Way to Live

"I began a new life with harmonious way to live,

I will master my desires and emotions with harmonious understanding,

I will persist on my path until I succeed with harmonious intentions, harmonious speech, harmonious actions and harmonious effort,

I will serve humanity with harmonious livelihood,

I will live in the present moment with harmonious mindfulness and harmonious concentration,

I have found a harmonious way to live."

"Happy is the man who could find a better way
to live his life with a harmonious way."

Part Two

The Harmonious Way to Live

The Harmonious Way to Live is an invitation to live in a mindful, peaceful and happy way, creating the conditions for an open heart and a wise mind. It is the sacred "Noble Eightfold Path" of harmony through Lord Buddha's wisdom, and it can be reached by cultivating morality, tranquility and wisdom. With a goal of transforming lives to be more meaningful and purpose-driven, one should live by principles of harmony, kindness and non-harming; it is the way for a peaceful world. This is the way to awaken your Buddha Nature here on Earth.

Harmonious Understanding

Harmonious understanding is an understanding of the universal truths through acquired wisdom. It is an aspect of ourselves that can be developed through a profound and thorough investigation into life.

Harmonious understanding is seeing things as they are, giving rise to a mind free from delusion. Harmonious understanding should change the way we look upon the world so we may see it as it truly is - interdependent yet unified. This understanding can assist us to move forward towards a peaceful future and enlightenment. This type of understanding becomes our ground for insight into things as they truly are; it is an understanding that moves beyond perception, perspective and belief.

It requires a degree of faith, however slight, to remember that even as we discover life to be inevitably disappointing, happiness is attainable. Awareness of impermanence, suffering and non self are crucial components of this contentment.

Harmonious Intention

Harmonious intention is the source of harmonious action; what we think initiates what we do and say. Man is made or unmade by himself and by the expanse of his intentions. If one has intentions which are kind and serene, harmonious speech and action will follow (and so too happiness) as surely and as closely as one's shadow. A man can only rise, awaken, and conquer by lifting up his thoughts.

"Thought in the mind hath made us. What we are by thought was wrought and built. If a man's mind hath evil thoughts, pain comes on him as comes the wheel the ox behind ......

if one endure sin purity of thought, joy follows him

As his own shadow- sure."

Harmonious intention is the fostering of selflessness and boundless love for all beings in our mind, and this love is then manifested as concern for the well-being of all life-forms. It is important to keep our hearts open and observe people and phenomena deeply before we pass judgment; thinking of other people or things as obstacles in our life can create division and conflict.

Harmonious intention is renouncing thoughts of ill will and cultivating skillful intentions of loving kindness, compassion and harmlessness.

Living with boundless love, compassion and harmlessness is choice available to all, regardless of religious beliefs, and deciding to follow the path of mindfulness alongside these principles is the greatest liberation.

Man is the master of intentions, the molder of character, the maker and shaper of his environment and the conditions of his final liberation.

When we cultivate loving states of awareness, we inevitably find there to be far more that bonds us than divides us, and through this discovery we feel more connected. No matter what our beliefs, cultural values, skin colour, race, actions, or status, we are joined together in this world through strands of relationship and interconnection. We must not forget the unity of humankind. We need to stop reinforcing the sense of "us", "them", "here" and "there"; the suffering child that we see in my motherland Sri Lanka is part of our lives. Nothing isolated happens anymore – not war, not disease, not an exploitation of the worker, not climate change, not the hope for something better; the environmental pollution happening in these faraway places is affecting your neighbourhood. This is the reason we must be environmentally consciousness.

Science shows that kindness towards others in need can provide a buffer against stress, and kindness towards ourselves can culminate in an increased sense of well-being. The attitude of loving kindness is inherent in a meaningful and beautiful life.

Boundless love is a universal teaching of the heart and mind that can unite a world. It is the great remover of tension, the great peace-maker in social conflict, and the healer of wounds suffered in the struggle of existence.

Radiating Boundless Love

Find a posture that helps you remain relaxed and alert.

First begin by sending loving kindness to yourself, and allowing your hearts to become open to others.

Use the following phrases:

May I be safe,

May I be happy,

May I be healthy,

May I live with ease.

Sense the love flowing through your heart, perhaps in a rhythm with the breath. Keep feeling that loving kindness.

After directing loving kindness to yourself, you move on to someone you find inspiring, or to whom you feel grateful. Bring the person's presence into your mind and direct the loving phrases toward him or her:

May you be safe,
May you be happy,
May you be healthy,
May you live with ease.

In the final phase we offer loving kindness to all beings everywhere. You may sense this loving kindness like a warmth or light. Feel how the boundless love flowing outwards from your heart is not specific to any one person but to all people.

Take a few minutes to explore extending your boundless love to the billions of people living on earth. Your universal loving kindness is extending to all living beings on this earth and other planets and to the whole universe.

May all beings be safe,
May all beings be happy,
May all beings be healthy,
May all beings live with ease.

Imagine living your life with the intention of transforming every interaction into an opportunity to increase goodwill towards others. Loving-kindness is that intention; it is the capacity to offer joy, goodwill, and happiness to another without expecting anything in return. These feelings can often be easier to experience than to describe. Loving kindness is boundless, open, spacious, and overflowing. A continuous loving kindness practice begins with unconditional love and acceptance, honing the natural human ability to be compassionate and caring. It results in numerous health benefits in relation to the wellbeing it creates within. The beauty of this practice is that you can bring it with you anywhere – at home, to work, even on vacation. As you bring loving kindness into your life, you begin to create a sense of connectedness not only to your own heart, but also to the beauty of life itself.

In loving kindness we may have discovered one of the most important ingredients of happiness; to increase your happiness, all you have to do is wish somebody else to be happy. That is all. It is a life changing experience.

Being a messenger of loving kindness is always the best way to receive love ourselves. Others will be drawn to the energy of this loving kindness: a warm smile, words of appreciation, sweet attention, and affection. Deep within, you are ultimately love itself.

Watering the seed of loving kindness in ourselves and others is a beautiful way of living. This expression of selfless compassion serves the betterment of humankind, while conditional, selfish love is the root of all the violence, injustice, and discontent humanity has experienced. We can see its influence in ourselves, in our family, in our society, in our country, and in the whole of humanity.

Hatred does not cease with hatred, but by love; this is the eternal rule.

When we truly understand this principle we become capable of spiritual growth. At this point it is possible to transform our lives, our work place, our family, our immediate society and the entire planet. Loving ourselves and loving others unconditionally is the purpose; this is living harmoniously.

"Like a mother who protects her child, her only child, with her own life, one should cultivate a heart of boundless love towards all living beings."

Compassion in Action

"We must all learn to live together as brothers or we will perish together."

None of us can live alone. We are dependent on one other, and so we must ascertain which components are needed in order to live in harmony together as brothers and sisters.

The answer is compassion.

The world suffers with its ever increasing busyness; we hardly notice the stranger in front of us. There are far more urgent things to pay attention to. The consequence of this distractedness is a lack of connection to the present moment. Whether it's a loved one, a stranger, or the person looking back at you in the mirror, you fail to notice the uniqueness and the needs of the human being in front of you. We must stay present and bring mindful attention to a world in need; this intention will open your mind and heart to the harmonious way. Mindfulness facilitates the experience of connection between ourselves and others. It is an experience of returning home to oneness and fullness.

Most men have their eyes and ears closed. They do not see the unbroken stream of tears flowing through life; they do not hear the cries of distress continually pervading the world. Bound by selfishness, their hearts have become hard and narrow. With a narrow heart, how can one strive for any higher purpose? They must realize that only a release from selfish craving can contribute to their own freedom from suffering.

It is compassion that removes the obstacles and opens the door to freedom; compassion makes the narrow heart as wide as the world.

Compassion has the power to reintroduce us to our own circumstances, showing us that the lives of others are often much harder than our own. Open your heart to glowing compassion.

The compassion of the wise man does not render him a victim of suffering. His thoughts, words, and deeds are full of empathy. His heart does not waver; it remains unchanged, serene and calm. Compassion is a beautiful quality of intellect and the heart, which knows, understands, and is eager to help. Compassion is strength and gives strength; the highest manifestation of compassion is to show the world the path which leads to the end of suffering.

Compassion is concern for the wellbeing of others and desiring for them to be free from all suffering and causation. Compassion is closely related to loving kindness. Both qualities pursue an end goal for all living beings to achieve happiness and peace.

Compassion applies to all areas of our lives. On a personal level, it is crucial to direct compassion towards ourselves, towards our friends and family, towards our colleagues and our boss, and even towards the people who sometimes disturb us; on a community level, the feeling and demonstration of compassion between one group and an other; on an international level, compassion of one nation for the citizens of other nations. If we do not care for others, all of us will suffer.

Compassion is the opposite of self-centeredness: the consistent desire to get the best and most for ourselves in order to ensure our own happiness. Our own self-centeredness does not benefit those around us, and as their problems will disturb not their tranquillity but eventually our own as well, there is truly no one benefiting from such selfishness.

Although we may appear to win small arguments, caring only for ourselves and humiliating and ignoring the misery of other people will eventually come back to us; the universal "Law of Karma" will ensure it. Therefore, to be happy it is essential to care for the welfare of others; rather than categorizing certain people as enemies whose needs are trivial, we must stay actively concerned with their well-being. When we respect them as our fellow human beings, helping them meet their basic needs, there will be no need for enemies. An enemy will become a friend.

Human beings are more dependent on each other now than in any other time in human history. Many of us do not know how much we depend on each other: those who make the roads we drive on, those who invent the technology we use, and those who teach us everything we know. Once we recognize our interconnectedness, society asks us to be responsive to the needs of others; to understand that by taking care of others we are consequently taking care of ourselves. Realizing that everyone and everything influences their surroundings highlights the breadth of this interconnection, and is a call to show compassion towards all other beings. Respecting this interconnection can open us to an honest and mindful life with compassion; we respect the choices of others, and we are ready to help them help themselves.

We cannot avert our eyes while looking at those who suffer, those who are hungry, ill or frightened. Our conception of life must include concern for everybody, and also everything in the environment. Environmental awareness helps us realize there is no "us" and "them." What happens "over there" has a direct effect on what happens to us "over here."

We see that caring for each other is more crucial than ever before. We have exceptional human brains, different from other species, so we have a duty to use our intelligence to help each other. This will enable all of us to benefit and live together peacefully. Compassion is the way to do this.

Bringing Compassion into the World

A mistake can provoke self-blame and shame, or it can be treated with kindness and compassion. Any trait we see in ourselves or others, any emotional storm, any experience of life's difficulties can be responded to in many different ways. One response we can work to consciously cultivate is compassion, outwardly and towards ourselves. Compassion involves recognizing the suffering of others and ourselves, allowing us to use our own pain and the pain of others as a vehicle for connection. It requires the willingness to observe negative thoughts and emotions with openness and clarity, so they can be evaluated authentically. Attentiveness is a non-judgmental, receptive state of mind in which one observes thoughts and feelings as they are, without trying to change or suppress them. We cannot ignore pain and work to develop compassion for it at the same time. Development of compassion, through the cultivation of awareness and loving kindness, is the surest way overcome life's inevitable frustrations, mistakes, and disappointments. As a force, love always holds the potential to flourish and help our lives flourish. As we meet with ups and downs in life and are showered with praise or criticism, always within these situation exists the ability of love without expectation. Life is so precarious; it shifts from pleasure to pain, ease to difficult confrontations, from getting exactly what we want to watching what we worked for begin to fade away. We must remember that even those who appear to have more than us suffer. The path is in front of us: rejoice in the happiness of others; love everyone and everything unconditionally; open your heart to understand the suffering of others and, armed with this power of compassion, give your heart to others unconditionally.

Consider a situation in the world in general or in your own life that could be improved by compassion. Imagine how the situation would be different if the people involved felt, thought, and acted with compassion.

"May you be free of your pain and sorrow."
"May you find peace."

Ahimsa - The Seed of Peace

The world does not know that we must all come to an end here; but those who know it, their quarrels cease at once.

Ahimsa is a non-harming and peaceful practice born out of understanding, love, compassion and equanimity. As a person born in Sri Lanka, I was introduced to the practice of *ahimsa* from my early childhood. From an early age I took care to harm no ant nor mosquito, and because I lived as a practitioner of this simple and respectful way of life, I later became a vegetarian. This peaceful way of living was the underlying principle of Gandhi's revolution and of his personal meditation practice. It is a good way to relate to the world and to create peace within yourself. It is incredibly rewarding to live without harming any living being; if we lived that way each moment, we wouldn't be experiencing the immense levels of violence we see in the world today. Perhaps equally as important, we would be more forgiving and less violent toward ourselves as well. During times when the world is at in conflict, with threats towards one other as extreme as the use of nuclear energy, *ahimsa* is the counteraction: the positive energy that can change the world. You can begin practicing *ahimsa* with yourself and move towards incorporating this way of being into your interactions with others in each and every moment of your mindful life.

The willingness to harm or hurt is ultimately born out of fear, which is evident in world politics today. Non-harming requires you to see your own fears and weaknesses and to understand them and own them mindfully. Again, this state of self awareness is most easily accessed with the mindful cultivation of loving kindness, compassion and equanimity. *Ahimsa* is the way to World Peace.

"If you can't love your enemy,
Start with your wife, or husband, or your children,
In each moment, strive to put their welfare first and
your own last, and let the circle of your love expand
from there."

Harmonious Speech

Despite all the technological advances in the modern world, effective communication between individuals can often be very difficult. Harmonious speech is concerned with establishing productive and honest communication that is beneficial to both the speaker and the listener; remaining aware of the potential suffering caused by unmindful speech and the refusal to listen to others. Committing to respectful speech and deep listening has the power to bring joy and happiness to others and relieve them of their suffering.

Harmonious speech is abstaining from false speech, abstaining from slanderous speech, abstaining from harsh speech, abstaining from idle chatter and determining the appropriate time for speech; ascertaining whether it is both useful and truthful.

Harmonious speech should be timely, truthful, gentle, kind and helpful. Failure to speak harmoniously is unwise and harmful, while telling the truth is a demonstration of care for other people.

Speech can break lives, create enemies, and start wars. We will receive the karma of our speech.

"All beings are the owners of their deeds, the heirs of their deeds; their deeds are the womb from which they spring. Whatever deeds they do - good or evil - of such they will be the heirs."

This is true with all the factors of moral virtue, speech, action and livelihood.

With harmonious speech, words are a treasure that should be divulged when they are useful and when the time is right. Harmonious speech requires the use of truthful and loving words, those intended to inspire self-confidence, joy and hope in others. It is about learning to listen deeply and understand when not to speak; this affords us the opportunity to find the "right" thing to say, the loving and supportive words that may serve to lessen the burdens of others.

Harmonious Action

A way to investigate our actions is to look at their aftereffects and the fruits they have produced. Becoming mindful of our bodily words and actions will allow us to more clearly recognize the spectrum of negative and positive outcomes. To practice harmonious action earnestly, it is essential to investigate the intentions behind our actions. Donating time and material resources to those in need is a true act of compassion; it will bring joy to yourself and others. These are harmonious actions.

Harmonious action is living according to guidelines: abstaining from taking life, abstaining from taking what is not freely given, abstaining from false speech, abstaining from sexual misconduct and abstaining from abusing mind-altering substances.

Every action has the potential to cause pain.

Every single thing we do has potential consequences that may echo far beyond what we can imagine. We should act carefully, as everything matters. Good intentions and actions can never produce bad results; bad thoughts and actions will not produce good results. That is to say nothing can come from corn but corn, nothing from nettles but nettles. Men seem to understand this law in the natural world and work within its confines, while few understand its relevance in the mental and moral world.

Harmonious Livelihood

Our vocation can support our efforts to live in a harmonious way and in the spirit of awakening. Having a harmonious livelihood is precious.

Supporting ourselves through work that is legal and peaceful is an effort to reduce harm to others. Specifically, we are not to trade in arms or lethal weapons, intoxicants or poisons, or to kill any living beings. Harmonious livelihood is based on wholesomeness.

Harmonious livelihood is concerned with ensuring that one earns one's living in a righteous way. Wealth should be gained in accordance with certain standards: one should acquire it by legal means, peacefully and without violence; one should acquire it honestly; one should acquire it in ways which do not cause harm or suffering for others.

Life is not about being rich, being popular, being highly educated or being perfect. Life is about being humble, kind, and willing to serve the world in a harmless way. In harmonious livelihood, every action is a sacred act to celebrate. Giving with the expectation of some reward will lead to anger and resentment – a vastly different outcome from offering a genuine labor of love. The latter is giving from the heart without expectation. When our incentive is primarily for money, or to achieve higher status, we are unlikely to find genuine fulfillment. Fulfillment comes from finding what you truly love to do, and directing all your energy towards it. When we learn to give from our own virtue with positive and harmonious intentions, we can experience the deep fulfillment of living a mindful and purposeful life.

Harmonious Effort

Harmonious effort means to live a life with the spirit of awakening. Harmonious effort is diligent action or thought that leads to spiritual freedom. A person driven by purpose knows that strength is developed through effort and exertion, adding effort to effort, patience to patience, and strength to strength; this person will grow divinely strong.

"One must think harmoniously, attempt doubtlessly and accomplish masterfully."

Your mind may be likened to a garden, intelligently cultivated or allowed to run wild. If no useful seeds are planted, an abundance of useless weeds will grow therein and will continue to produce their kind.

Just as a gardener cultivates his plot – keeping

it free from weeds and growing the flowers and fruits which he requires – so may you tend the garden of your mind. It is possible to weed out the wrong, useless and unwholesome thoughts through harmonious effort.

Harmonious effort need not be a struggle. It is a balance practice of ease and care. It is striving to awaken and strengthen wholesome mental states and to renounce unwholesome ones. The terms wholesome and unwholesome are used to mean that which leads to happiness and that which leads to unhappiness.

We have a choice regarding our state of mind. Thoughts and emotions can be transformed through harmonious effort; we can replace one with another. Bursts of greed and anger, which are natural responses to pleasant and unpleasant experiences, can be replaced with wholesome states of detachment and love through harmonious effort.

There are four functions to harmonious effort.

The first is to overcome the unwholesome seeds that have already been planted in our minds. When feelings of hate and aggression enter our consciousness, we must remember to practice present moment awareness. We should not allow these emotions to pull us into actions that we will regret. If we practice mindful breathing and allow the emotional reaction to pass, we can work to stave off the path of suffering.

Letting go of unwholesome mental states is complemented by a second function of harmonious effort: preventing unwholesome seeds from manifesting in the mind through calm reflection and insight.

The third function of the harmonious effort is to cultivate and actively tend to the wholesome seeds in the mind. Wholesome seeds are those that bring us peace, joy and freedom on a spiritual level. Living simply, taking time to enjoy life, and appreciating our loved ones are steps one can take towards these states of mind. Wholesome states of mind can be categorized in various ways – serenity and insight, the four foundations of mindfulness, the eight factors of the harmonious path, seven factors of enlightenment etc. The seven factors of enlightenment are, mindfulness, investigation of phenomena, energy, rapture, tranquility, concentration and equanimity; these factors lead to enlightenment and constitute enlightenment.

Once wholesome seeds have bloomed in our mind, we can turn to the final function of harmonious effort: sustaining the seeds we have successfully cultivated. We can keep them strong in our mind by nourishing them with mindfulness and concentration. Breathing in and out with mindful awareness is an ever constant light of peace that brings ease and contentment.

Harmonious Mindfulness

———— ◈ ————

Harmonious mindfulness refers to the practice of nonjudgmental attention – mental action that does not label or conceptualize.

"Mindfulness is paying attention on purpose in the present moment non-judgmentally."

It is sometimes called "appropriate attention." Our attention can often wander from the present moment, and so we must practice bringing it back with harmonious attention. This attentiveness requires becoming adept at noticing body, feelings, states of mind and mind objects; it becomes an authentic acceptance of the present experience. It is being open to and receiving the present moment as it is, pleasant or unpleasant, without clinging to or rejecting it. As you start to become more aware from moment to moment, the fundamental truth of life's experience will present themselves as insights.

As this insight grows, the habitual mental clinging to what is temporary will diminish, and with it suffering will also lessen.

Exercise

Practice of Four Foundations of Mindfulness - The Way to Liberation

Mindfulness of the Body

Find a comfortable place that allows for complete relaxation. Become aware of your immediate environment. Ask yourself the following

What am I seeing? Colors, shapes, beauty?

What I am hearing? Birds, people, cars?

What is happening in my body in this moment? Notice your quality of breath - if you have pain, tension in muscles, and your level of relaxation.

Be mindful about in-and-out breathing, the four elements, the parts of the body, bodily postures (walking, standing, sitting, and lying), etc.

Mindfulness of feelings

What feelings do you experience? Notice if they are pleasant, unpleasant, or neutral.

Mindfulness of consciousness

Notice states of consciousness: wholesome, unwholesome or indeterminate.

Mindfulness of Mind Objects

A range of mental and material phenomena, including certain hindrances to mindfulness (sensual desires, ill-will, dullness of mind, restlessness and worry, doubt), the five aggregates (body, feelings, perceptions, mental formations and consciousness), the factors of enlightenment (mindfulness, investigation, energy joy, tranquility, concentration, equanimity), the Noble Truths, etc.

Mindfulness is a way to experience the gift of the present moment – a process of deepening our sensitivity to the seemingly ordinary activities of life. For example, we devote time

every day to nourish our body, to prepare
food and to eat it. These often automatic
activities can become moments of deep
appreciation and awareness. We can adopt the
discipline of mindful eating – making an effort
to always sit down to eat, approaching this
activity calmly and slowly and with an
intention to be fully present. We can choose to
bring mindful attention to the taste and
sensations of each piece of food that is being
consumed. Being aware of your posture and
ensuring the body is relaxed and at ease is
important. As well, feeling grateful to the
people and the environment that made each
piece of food possible.

*Be aware that the food you eat will cause no harm to
you or any other living being.*

"Wake up my friend, to save yourself, your
families, children, animals, and everything
you feel is worth living for by mindful
harmless eating. This means eating whole
foods – a plant-based diet. Consciously

cultivate well-being and harmony in those ordinary moments, awakening joy in each mouthful of food.

"Mindful eating can bring a lot of joy and increase the chances for survival of life on earth."

Beautiful Breath

It is the nature of mind to wander and react to external stimuli. By training yourself to focus on something simple and repetitive like the breath, and being prepared to retrieve your attention when begins to stray from the object of focus, you become better at noticing. You can be anywhere in the world - from the busiest streets of New York to a quiet cave in the Himalayas - and still remain aware of your beautiful breath. Training the mind to be more aware of the breath can not only help you remain grounded in moments of stress, but can also improve your focus and concentration at work and home.

This mindful breathing is a gentle workout for your attention; with practice it will become easier and you will be able to focus for longer periods of time. This simple practice is an antidote for stress, anxiety, restlessness, and could lead to states of insight and relaxation. Learning how to become intimate with the breath can widen the space between stimulation and response, allowing us to break away from bad habits and open up to the freedom to truly pay attention to the wonders all around us.

Attending to the breath evokes the body's relaxation response by calming the mind and allowing it to gently focus on what is happening in the present moment. Your only responsibility is to concentrate on the sensation of each inhalation and exhalation, noticing when your attention has wandered and patiently returning it to the breath. That is all. When you become aware of distractions, you are mindful. This is the moment you can choose to return to again and again. As you intentionally practice coming back into the present moment, little by little you are cultivating a central attitude of the beautiful way. This is a powerful realization.

Make this meditation as much a part of your daily routine as brushing your teeth. Set aside five minutes, ten minutes or half an hour a day depending on your circumstances and experience.

Your posture should be erect and balanced but not stiff, with your head, neck, and back aligned. The aim is to be relaxed, alert, and reflecting upon your state of mind. You can practice sitting cross-legged on a cushion on the floor, or in a chair with your legs uncrossed and the soles of your feet flat on the floor.

Take a few slow, deep breaths. Relax your shoulders and facial muscles. Notice the points of contact between your body and the floor, cushion or chair. Now focus on the sensations of your breath at your nostrils as you breathe in and out. Do not try to control or change the breath, simply observe it. When you realize that your mind has wandered from the breath, notice what has happened and gently bring back your attention back to the breath. Limit your attention to each inhalation and exhalation as it comes. Focusing on the breath is your only responsibility, so you can let go of all other worries. If you are having trouble staying focused, count from 1 to 10 as you breathe in and out. You could also focus on a particular word or phrase. Once you have finished your meditation session, open your eyes, stretch and give yourself a few minutes before getting up and serving the world in an easy and relaxed way. This breathing meditation will open your mind to a state of attentiveness to the present moment and everything you do. Whether it is brushing your teeth, washing dishes, or eating lunch, all activities can be done mindfully.

It is a Miracle to Walk on Earth

Each of us is on a short journey on Earth. In the vast cosmological scheme, it is a rare and precious thing to be born as a human being on this planet.

To walk on earth is the greatest miracle in your life. Take this precious short time on earth to fully experience its beauty. Walk slowly and leisurely in a garden, along a river, along a farm, or on a village path. Be aware of the beauty around you. Notice freshness in the air you breathe, and see the wonder of light and shade as the sun shines through the leaves swaying in the breeze. Feel the sensation of your feet on ground and the miracle of walking on this earth.

Now direct the mind away from the scenery and focus it instead to the soles of your feet, on the sensations and feelings as they arise and pass away. As you walk, these sensations may change. As the foot lifts and comes into contact with different earth, a new feeling can arise. Become aware of this sensation on the sole of the foot. Again, as the foot lifts, evaluate the new feeling as it arises. When you lift each foot and place it down, familiarize yourself with the sensations you feel. At each step, new feelings arise and old feelings cease; we are aware of the types of feelings that arise at the soles of the feet. Concentrate on the heaviness and lightness on the feet as these are the fundamental sensations for insight. If you understand the impermanent nature of suffering and of objects of meditation, you will notice the importance of these characteristics. This is a type of attentive meditation called walking meditation, in which one can focus the mind and develop investigative knowledge and wisdom to awaken calmness and insight; it is a path to mental and physical well-being. As so much of life is taken up with the activity of walking, knowing how to apply awareness to this simple action can become a wonderful act of calming and insight. Lord Buddha spoke of five benefits of walking meditation: endurance for walking long distances, it is good for striving, it is healthy, it is good for the digestion after a meal, and the concentration acquired from a walking meditation lasts a long time. This wonderful act will help you to overcome drowsiness as it develops a heightened sense of alertness, effort, and zeal. We are bringing the mind to the here and now; you will start noticing the experience of walking more fully. Notice how you can develop happiness born of serenity as you are walking, and once your attention is fully focused on the experience of walking you will find it to be a very pleasant experience. As your awareness increases you will know more and more of the sensations of walking. Then you find that walking possesses a sense of beauty and peace to it. Every step becomes a "beautiful step". This will awaken peacefulness, a sense of stillness, a sense of the mind being at ease and happy in its own harmonious nature.

Harmonious Concentration

Harmonious concentration is developing one-pointed and skillful absorption for insight. It is the ability to direct the attention into one single thing. It produces qualities in the mind such as a sense of ease, balance and relaxation.

Concentration of mind is a beautiful jewel of wisdom; it is the result of long and patient efforts in self-control. This is a state of mind that is calm, serene, and relaxed – pointedly concentrated, stable and still. Its presence is an indication of a ripened experience, and of an extraordinary knowledge of laws and operations of thought. A man becomes calm insofar as he is able to understand himself. As he develops a harmonious understanding and sees things more clearly – the internal relation of things through cause and effect – he ceases to fuss and fume and worry and grieve but remains poised, steadfast, and serene with one-pointedness of mind. The more tranquil a man becomes, the greater is his goodness. The calm man is always loved and revered like a shade-giving tree in a thirsty land, or a sheltering rock in a storm. It does not matter whether it rains or shines, or what changes come to those possessing these blessings, for they remain sweet, serene and calm. That equanimity of character which we call tranquility is the last lesson of the path; it is the flowering of new life. It is as precious as wisdom and more desired than gold. How insignificant money worshiping looks in comparison with to a serene life of fulfillment – a life that dwells in the ocean of Truth, beneath the waves and beyond the reach of tempests, in the Harmonious Calm.

Humanity surges with uncontrolled passion and the affects of ungoverned grief; we are blown about by stress, anxiety and doubt. Only the purposeful wise man, whose thoughts are controlled and purified, can control the winds and storms of the illusionary self. Ultimately the concept of "self" falls away and he become one with his action. Also, the man who is big enough to be Somebody is also willing graciously accept status as Nobody; he is content to be one who has travelled the "Harmonious Path."

Wherever you are, whoever you be, under whatever conditions you may live, whatever belief system you follow, know this: in the ocean of life and the cycles of birth and death, the isles of blessedness are smiling and the sunny shore of your final liberation awaits you. The peaceful oasis is in sight if you are willing to follow "The Harmonious Path" – for your own spiritual enlightenment and also towards the betterment of humanity. Self-control is virtue; calmness is power; wisdom is mastery. Say unto your heart, "Peace, be still." Seek that peaceful world within you – the peaceful world that you create in your own mind.

"Curb your speech,
Restrain your mind,
Commit no evil deed,
By these means,
Accomplish the practices of the harmonious message,
And Create Peaceful World."

Daily Reflections for

Harmonious Living

For one of harmonious understanding, harmonious intention originates. For one of harmonious intention, harmonious speech originates. For one of harmonious speech, harmonious action originates. For one of harmonious action, harmonious livelihood originates. For one of harmonious livelihood, harmonious effort originates. For one of harmonious effort, harmonious mindfulness originates. For one of harmonious mindfulness, harmonious concentration originates. For one of harmonious concentration, harmonious knowledge originates. For one of harmonious knowledge, harmonious liberation originates.

- From Teachings of Lord Buddha

Today I will master my desires and emotions with harmonious understanding

Harmonious understanding is seeing things as they are, giving rise to a mind free from delusion. Harmonious understanding should change the way we look upon the world so we may see it as it truly is by understanding the four noble truths (understanding suffering, understanding the origin of suffering; understanding the extinction of suffering, understanding the path that leads to the extinction of suffering.), understanding the wholesome and unwholesome, understanding the three characteristics of existence, that all formations are impermanent, that all formations subject to suffering, that everything is not self. This understanding can assist us to move forward towards a peaceful future and enlightenment. This type of understanding becomes our ground for insight into things as they truly are; it is an understanding that moves beyond perception, perspective and belief.

Today I will persist on my path until I succeed with harmonious intentions

Harmonious intention is renouncing thoughts of ill will and cultivating skillful intentions of loving kindness, compassion and harmlessness.

Today I will persist on my path until I succeed with harmonious speech

Harmonious speech is abstaining from false speech, abstaining from slanderous speech, abstaining from harsh speech, abstaining from idle chatter and determining the appropriate time for speech; ascertaining whether it is both useful and truthful.

Today I will persist on my path until I succeed with harmonious action

Harmonious action is living according to guidelines: abstaining from taking life, abstaining from taking what is not freely given, abstaining from false speech, abstaining from sexual misconduct and abstaining from abusing mind-altering substances.

Today I will serve humanity with harmonious livelihood

Supporting ourselves through work that is legal and peaceful is an effort to reduce harm to others. Specifically, we are not to trade in arms or lethal weapons, intoxicants or poisons, or to kill any living beings. Harmonious livelihood is based on wholesomeness.

Today I will persist on my path until I succeed with harmonious effort

Harmonious effort need not be a struggle. It is a balance practice of ease and care. It is striving to awaken and strengthen wholesome mental states and to renounce unwholesome ones. The terms wholesome and unwholesome are used to mean that which leads to happiness and that which leads to unhappiness.

Today I will live in the present moment with harmonious mindfulness

"Mindfulness is paying attention on purpose in the present moment non-judgmentally."

It is sometimes called "appropriate attention." Our attention can often wander from the present moment, and so we must practice bringing it back with harmonious attention. This attentiveness requires becoming adept at noticing body, feelings, states of mind and mind objects; it becomes an authentic acceptance of the present experience. It is being open to and receiving the present moment as it is, pleasant or unpleasant, without clinging to or rejecting it. As you start to become more aware from moment to moment, the fundamental truth of life's experience will present themselves as insights.

Today I will live in the present moment with harmonious concentration

Harmonious concentration is developing one-pointed and skillful absorption for insight. It is the ability to direct the attention into one single thing. It produces qualities in the mind such as a sense of ease, balance and relaxation.

Harmonious Reflections

"The best of ways is the eightfold."

Harmonious Understanding

"Harmonious understanding is the forerunner of the harmonious way to live, that leads to lasting peace."

Harmonious Intentions

"All that we are is the result of what we have thought."

Harmonious Speech

"If a man speaks with a pure thought, happiness
follows him."

Harmonious Action

"The virtuous man delights in this world, and he delights in the next, he delights in both."

Harmonious Livelihood

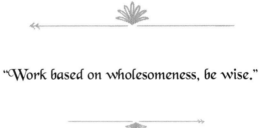

"Work based on wholesomeness, be wise."

Harmonious Effort

"The wise always possessed of harmonious effort
attain the highest happiness."

Harmonious Mindfulness

"Moment-to-moment mindfulness helps you avoid regrettable actions and will lead to final liberation."

Harmonious Concentration

"Concentrate on wholesome thoughts and actions."

May you be Safe,

May you be Healthy,

May you be Happy,

May you be at Ease.

May all beings be Safe,

May all beings be Healthy,

May all beings be Happy,

May all beings be at Ease.

About the Author

Jayan E. Romesh is an engineer turned author, inspiring and touching hearts with his simple and unique teachings on loving kindness, compassion, forgiveness, peace, happiness, mindfulness, enlightenment and harmonious living. His books Happiness Now, Art of Loving Kindness and Path Less Traveled have touched the lives of many.

Jayan is the founder of Metta Library publishers, and is striving to carry out his harmonious efforts to make this world a better and more peaceful place for all beings through his principles of harmonious living.

Born and raised in Sri Lanka, Jayan resides in Vancouver, Canada.

Thank You For Reading Harmonious Way to Live. I really appreciate all of your feedback, and I love hearing what you have to say. I need your input to make the next version better. Please leave me a helpful review on Amazon letting me know what you thought of the book. If you enjoyed the book,

You'll want to visit, www.mettalibrary.com
Where you can read many more!
And while you're there,
Be sure to request,
Free books, meditations and email newsletter
So you can:
Be the first to read my latest writings,
Receive updates on when my next book is available,
Receive guidance to write your own enlightening book,
Information about online trainings,
And much more!
Thanks so much, with Love and Blessings!! ~
Jayan E. Romesh

40094609R00064

Made in the USA
Middletown, DE
25 March 2019